TI0666940

© 2008 by Judy Pigott and John W. Gibson (Taking Flight Through Life, LLC)

ISBN 13: 978-0-9779226-7-3 (workbook)
ISBN 13: 978-0-9779226-5-9 (workbook–downloadable)

Printed in the United States of America

Editor: Karen Parkin
Cover illustration: Stu Heinecke
Design: Annie Vasquez Design

Our workbook is intended to be a guide, support, and reference for you as you weave your personal safety net of plans, people, and resources. We've designed this workbook to complement our book, Personal Safety Nets®, and to be used by both individuals and organizations or groups. All contents are protected by copyright by Taking Flight Through Life, LLC.

Personal Safety Nets®

Workbook

Your Personal Safety Net: People, Plans, and Resources

Insert a photo of you
and your personal safety net.

This is the Personal Safety Nets® plan for ___Joyce Palazzo___ ,
as of ___June 2009___ , to be revisited at major life changes or every five
years, whichever comes first.

Safety Nets Unlimited

Judy Pigott and Dr. John W. Gibson

Our Vision:

We envision a world where each of us experiences care, creativity, and connection through interwoven personal safety nets. We see a future in which each of us has several people and solid plans to turn to in times of change or challenge, expected or unexpected, planned or unplanned.

Our Mission:

To teach, support, reinforce, and demonstrate the power of choice, connection, and intentional outreach to others as ways of increasing resourcefulness, resiliency, and renewal. To increase the security, safety, and cohesiveness of ourselves and our communities.

Our Values:

Effectiveness can always be enhanced by preparation and practice

Learning happens throughout all of life and can be planned

Community is essential to happiness and longevity and part of strength

Kindness can come from unexpected quarters and helps us all

Security is enhanced through connection with others

Power is being able to see and effect choices and ask for help

Hope is a cornerstone of strength

Humor smooths the bumps, raises the spirits, and heals

Strength in community

Every prophet sought out companions.

A wall standing alone is useless

But put three or four walls together,

And they'll support a roof and keep

The grain dry and safe.

When ink joins with a pen, then the blank paper

Can say something. Rushes and reeds must be woven

To be useful as a mat. If they weren't interlaced,

The wind would blow them away.

Like that, God paired up

Creatures, and gave them friendship.

—*Rumi*

Found in *The Fragrance of Faith* by Jamal Rahman, The Book Foundation, Bath, England, 2004. Originally from Mathnawi VI: 518-523, Barks and Moyne, *The Essential Rumi*, p. 247

Table of Contents

Personal Safety Nets Information
Chapters 1 – 3

Introduction   p. 6

1. What Do I Know Right Now?   p. 8

2. Identifying Safety Net Members   p. 14

3. Asking and Organizing   p. 22

Gathering Data
Chapters 4 – 6

4. Collecting Home and Family Information   p. 30

5. Nitty-Gritty of Your Life   p. 34

6. Planning for Emergencies   p. 56

Team in Action
Chapters 7 – 8

7. Pulling Your Team Together   p. 58

8. Maintaining Your Team   p. 74

Congratulations and Conclusion   p. 80

Appendix and Order Form

5

> *Success is the sum of the confident decisions you make.*
> *—Unknown*

Introduction

This workbook will help you build a strong, dependable community in preparation for unexpected changes, challenges, and opportunities.

You will also gather important information, identify your team, and decide how you will invite them.

While creating your team, you might feel like the following:

Director
General manager
Expedition leader
Sergeant
Choreographer
CEO
Matriarch or patriarch

You might think of your team members as:

Community
Family
Buddies
Mentors
Recruits
Advisors
Cast

How to use this workbook

In our book *Personal Safety Nets*, our goal was to explain the concepts of creating and using personal safety nets. We also added life to those concepts by providing many real-life examples of real people engaged in various aspects of creating and/or managing personal safety nets and of a personal safety net (PSN) in action.

We've designed this workbook to be used with our book, *Personal Safety Nets*. Our goal is to guide and inspire you to create your own personal safety net or team and to know how to call your PSN into action when needed.

This workbook is a simple guide for all who find themselves needing to receive assistance or to be a part of a PSN team. This guide could also be used by a spouse, partner, or friend of someone needing help. This workbook is packed with ideas, examples and tools designed to help you more effectively deal with changes, challenges and opportunities.

In *Personal Safety Nets* we provided observations and shared experiences and examples about boundaries, setting limits, and personal choice and responsibility. We invite you to keep issues and potential stumbling blocks in mind while getting involved in the nuts and bolts of PSN creation and PSN team activities.

As you use this workbook, or modify it for your needs and own life circumstance, it's important to always keep in mind that the tools are to support and enhance the life of the PSN care partner and the lives of those on the PSN team. Tools and forms have a way of becoming ends unto themselves–don't let this happen.

Again, it's your personal safety net. We provide you with ideas, but the choices, decisions, and adaptations of these ideas are up to you. You, and your experts, consultants, friends, and family create, and forever modify and update, your personal safety net.

6

Thoughts for next steps:

Help!
Who can you turn to?

Consider who would help you if one of these situations came about. These people are the basis of your safety net team.

If you fall off your skateboard, who'll feed your cat?

What if this happened to you?

Story 1: Seth, a 27-year-old financial planner, suffered a serious concussion and head injury during a weekend soccer game. He was unable to think clearly enough to make decisions or drive for three weeks.

- Who would be called?
- Is she/he authorized to speak for you?
- Does she/he know of your plan?

Story 2: Sarah, a divorced woman with no siblings, was injured in a car accident while returning from her daily visit with her elderly parents. She suffered injuries that required several surgeries and weeks in the hospital.

- Who would be called?
- Who will visit you?
- Who will visit Mom?

Story 3: Bill and Marty's SUV skidded on ice and rolled several times. Both were injured and remained in critical condition in an out-of-state hospital. Their three children, ages 7, 13, and 15, were staying with various friends.

- If you couldn't take care of your children, who would?
- Do they know this?
- Have you taken legal steps to authorize them?

CHAPTER ONE

Life is 10% what happens to you and 90% what you do with it.
—Unknown

What do I know right now?

How do I begin?

Here is an outline on how this workbook approaches gathering information and creating a safety net.

1. **Personal/emotional:**
   Unless this is strong, the rest may fall apart–nothing else matters!

   - Who are my friends? Who could I most likely count on?

   - To whom do/would I turn for various kinds of support?

   - Who'd be called first in an emergency? What would they need to know? Have I told them? In an emergency, how would someone else know who to call?

2. **Community:**

   - Organizations that help or support me

   - Specific or categories of places I can/do turn to

(Continued on page 9)

1. Personal/emotional resources: *family*

   Gloria Groff

   Carolyn Lorang

   Jon Nahr

   Katy Durbin

2. Community resources:

   St Brendan's Parish

   Evergreen Health Center

   Tuesday Scripture Group

Notes on next steps to take:

Knowledge is power.

Creating a safety net is emotional protection from life's endless disruptions. It also involves ordering your affairs, taking stock, building community, and enhancing life.

In this workbook, we have created a web of plans, resources, systems and people who, together, give meaning, support and ease to your life.

3. Medical resources: *Dr. Connie Smith 425-899-6800*

Carol Van Haelst 425-899-3181

4. Insurance resources: *Medicare / Aetna*

Auto - Pemco

5. Legal resources: *Will   Power of Attorney*

6. Financial resources: *Boeing Credit Union*

US Bank

7. Legacy: _____

3. Medical:
- History
- Current primary doctor
- Allergies
- Medications

4. Insurance:
- Life
- Auto/home
- Medical
- Other

5. Legal:
- Will
- Ethical will
- Plans for funeral
- Affairs in order

6. Financial:
- What is my bank? Who is my banker?
- What is my local branch?
- What is my credit union?

7. Legacy:
- What will I be remembered for?
- Do I have any opinion on where or how I'm buried or remembered?

Getting started

Some people already have a personal safety net structure. We believe there's value in not only having a structure, but also in knowing that you do. Here is the beginning of a plan.

How will I use this workbook?

Some of you will start at the beginning and systematically go forward.

Some of you will start where you think it would be most fun to start.

Others might want to start where you have the least information and get the hardest done first.

But, no matter what, start!

- Carry ID with you.

- Have names of top three personal safey net contacts on this card and their numbers in your cell phone (see page 56).

Think about and try to answer these questions

1. General questions:

- What might be needed?

- What's in place? What is missing?

- How do I ask for help? What do I say?

Carry ID with me !

Have personal safety net contacts on my cell phone !

Notes:

10

Life happens—are you ready?

You gain strength, courage, and confidence by every experience in which you really stop to look fear in the face.

—Eleanor Roosevelt

2. Specific questions:

- Where are my important papers?
- Where is the key to my safe deposit box?
- What's the password to my email address list?
- Where is the spare key to my house? Who else knows this?

1. Contact Jim Palazzo who is my Power of attorney.

Personal safety nets create emotional protection from life's endless disruptions— and more!

Community resources

Finances

Family

Legal system

Spiritual guides

Philosophical bases

Health care professionals

Alternative medicine

Education/work/vocation

Hobbies/avocation

Volunteer work

Funeral plans/preferences

Legacy plans

Knowledge is power!

One kind of knowledge is knowing what resources you have, where they are, and how to reach them. This knowledge brings you power and strength.

Thinking ahead

Often it's wise to think ahead of time about some of the hard choices in life. Even if the thought of these things is dreadfully difficult, by thinking of them now you will make better choices when the need arises.

Why create a safety net?

Some people may have a safety net without knowing it.

We believe in the value of not only having a safety net but also knowing that you do. Knowing that you have a plan in place allows you to:

Feel safe and secure in an increasingly less predictable world.

Analyze the strengths and weaknesses of your safety net against probable changes—wanted and unwanted—and update, revise, and strategically strengthen it.

Increase your awareness of the need to protect, nourish, and savor your relationships with these people who are important to you.

12

Notes: _____

_____

_____

How will I use my personal safey net?

Creating a safety net ahead of time is useful in so many ways and situations. Here are a few:

◆ *Caring for an aging spouse or parent*

◆ *Looking ahead to surgery*

◆ *Experiencing a divorce or solo parenting*

◆ *Caring for a premature or ill child*

◆ *Living with a prolonged illness or through menopause*

◆ *Having some other change or challenge*

Any of these are made better by having one or more safety nets!

These same personal safety nets will enhance your life if you're just living life but want the increased assurance, peace, and intimacy that come from having, developing, and cultivating one.

Planning ahead can help you:

- Know when to ask for help
- Know what to ask for
- Understand how to pull a team together
- Recruit, organize, maximize, and utilize such a team
- Have documents you need at hand
- Sleep more soundly at night
- Know you are not alone
- Not "reinvent the wheel," but modify it to fit your needs

13

Organizing:
How to be more prepared

Every day I hear stories that remind me of the value of care teams and the value they give to human life...
—*Case manager*

You might be thinking, "If only I'd read this before...then we could have organized ourselves and been much more helpful. And not so stressed." Here are some tools so you and your team will be ready next time.

Making your safety net accessible

Here are some ways to create quick and easy access to your safety net team:

1. Enter all members in your cell phone; add ICE or PSN before each name so they are grouped together.

2. Put all members in your email address book.

3. Make an email group list of your PSN members.

4. Create and carry a phone tree, described on page 27.

Setting up a communication tree

Organization is the key.

In an emergency or a crisis, do you think you will call everyone yourself? Probably not, so:

Who gets called/emailed first?

If you use email, do you have a group email list set up? Think of who's on it.

- Is there one person who could be in charge of sending messages?
- Is there one tier (everyone who might be interested)?
- Are there several tiers (first the top 3 or 4 contacts, then friends and family who you want to be kept in the loop)?
- Is anyone to be left off?

If you've decided who is part of your personal safety net, are their names/numbers given special designation in your database and on your phone?

If you're phone-based, make a phone tree, making a copy for everyone, so that you, or someone on your inner "A"team, makes only one call—or two at the most, yet everyone is notified.

Notes:

26

Sample email list

Granny's team list: grannyteam@network.com:
Five names
- Bob: bobtsmith@network.com
- Lil: liligirl@network.com
- Mary: maryjones@network.com
- Tom: tomfarmer@network.com
- Jane: janedoe@network.com

Sample phone tree

Phone trees cut down the work of any one person. To send out information, call the first person on the tree. The first person, in turn, must make contact directly with someone next on the list. Call until you reach someone, then go back to make sure no one is missed. Voice or text messages aren't sufficient unless the message is pretty neutral or routine.

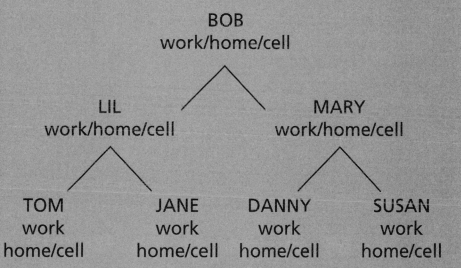

BOB
work/home/cell

LIL
work/home/cell

MARY
work/home/cell

TOM
work
home/cell

JANE
work
home/cell

DANNY
work
home/cell

SUSAN
work
home/cell

So, if Bob gets the first call, he calls Lil and Mary. But if, say, Lil isn't reachable, Bob calls Tom or Jane. Obviously it is of critical importance that this informantion be kept current, so the name of the coordinator (in this case, Bob) is on the sheet too.

Personal safety net access backup plan

It is important that at least one other person besides you be able to call your safety net into action or communicate directly with your safety net team in time of need.

Your spouse, partner, best friend, adult child, or person holding Power of Attorney (POA), etc., should have a hard copy of your plan, a phone list, and an email list.

Each member of your team should have a contact sheet or an email group list that includes all members.

Clear, simple, direct, tactful and consistent

When it's time to invite people to be part of your safety network, you'll want to try to be invitational and allow for "no".

Saying "yes!"

There are many ways you can say yes:

"Yes, I can help."

"Yes, I can help this Saturday."

"Yes, I'm not usually available on the weekends, but this Saturday is a rare exception and I can help."

"Yes, I can help this Saturday, but with my new job and my wife's illness, this may be the only time I can help."

Often when faced with a request, we are concerned about choosing "yes." You may be thinking:

"What am I getting myself into?"

"If I say 'yes' this time, will they keep asking?"

"If I say 'yes,' will they become dependent on me?"

Formalizing your safety net

Vera, I've been thinking about being proactive in my life, getting my affairs in order, you know, finally doing my will and such. Anyway, one thing I want is to have someone be my Power of Attorney, to take over my affairs for me if I were incapable. You're my closest, dearest friend, and I like the way you run your life. Would you be willing to take on this responsibility for me?

Sharee, I'd like to ask if you'd be one of the people I really can count on in a pinch. There's nothing going on right now that I know about, but I'm thinking that I'd like to have a network of people who know me pretty well, who know what's going on in my life, and to whom I can turn. Vera has said she'll be my Power of Attorney, and Quentin is there as backup. But I'd like to have two or three other people close by, and you're one of them. It's OK to say "no," but would you consider doing this for me? If so, we can set aside time to talk about more details.

Phillip, my mom is getting older. You've been a friend of hers for many years, and I know she sort of depends on you. Since you and she live far away from me, I'm wondering if you'd be willing to have me put you on a list of people I could call if she needs help?

28

Notes: _____

_____

_____

Five Web sites for keeping up to date with far-flung support groups:

www.carepages.com
www.caringbridge.com
www.supportteam.org
www.familynetwork.org
www.lotsofhelpinghands.com

When you've been asked to take part in holding someone's safety net, there are many ways in which you might respond. Here are a few possibilities.

Responding to an invitation

☐ Yes, I'd like to learn more about your personal safety net.

☐ Yes, I'd like to keep talking. This sounds like something I should know about.

☐ No. I like the idea and value our relationship, but I'm overextended right now. Can we put this off for a while? I'd like to get a copy of the book though. Where can I find it?

☐ Please take me off the list. I've no idea who you are!

Saying "no"

"I would really like to but . . ."

"I don't know what to say. I feel awkward, but that's something I just don't feel I can do."

"Another day would be fine, but today won't work."

"What I'm hearing you say is _____, and you may need to talk . . ."

Hearing and understanding "no" replies

"No" can be painful to hear. Many of us have developed a strong reaction to "no" based on our own disappointments and hurt when we've been on the receiving end. While we cannot totally control how someone will react to our words, we can learn ways to express "no" that will reduce the likelihood that the other person will feel hurt.

CHAPTER FOUR

Collecting Home and Family Information

Life itself will ensure that you experience surprises —some welcome and some not.

This might happen to:

- ☐ You
- ☐ Someone you love
- ☐ Someone you can help

You can choose to:

- ☐ Take charge
- ☐ Stay out of it
- ☐ Join or help form a team
- ☐ Get scared and retreat

Be sure to include the following:

1. Personal information from
   a. My personal files
   b. Community resources
   c. Friends and family or other important people
   d. Spiritual guides and those I turn to for counsel

2. Housing

3. Medical information and directives

4. Other insurance

5. Financial documents and information

6. Legal documents and information

7. Next stage plans and information

8. Emergency information and plans

30

Notes: _____

_____

_____

What can I offer to do?

Name: _____

Address: _____

Home phone: _____ Work phone: _____

Cell phone: _____ Email: _____

Availability: In general, what are the best days, times and ways for you to give help? What are your special gifts or what do you like to do that could be useful?

Carmella's story

At 10:45 a.m. Carmella's cell phone rang. Because she was at work, she looked at the number to see who was calling. Her husband. He knew she wasn't supposed to take calls now—so it must be an emergency.

And it was. A call from the fire department had told him that their house was on fire. He couldn't leave work, but he knew Carmella probably could. With kids at school, the house was empty. Could anything be saved?

Carmella ran home to find the house blocked off by emergency vehicles. Only their fireproof safe could be salvaged.

Do you have a safe place where your keep important documents?

Where is it?

What is in it?

In Carmella's safe, which was in the bedroom closet, were passports, birth and marriage certificates, and other important papers. All their possessions and photos were gone, but they were alive and had what they needed to start anew.

Inside your fireproof safe or safe deposit box:

- Passports and any other identity documents or copies
- Social security cards
- Birth/death certificates
- Marriage/divorce certificates
- Copies of important legal documents
- Information on finances/mortgages/insurances
- Passwords
- Extra keys
- Key information on health
- Extra prescriptions for life-threatening illnesses
- Other important documents or items

Special concerns about your home

Information for someone living in your house

It's good to be prepared for a time when someone else may be living in your home, such as an adult child, house sitter, elderly parent, foreign exchange student, or long-term tenant.

- Departure date/time
- Return date/time
- Dishwasher/soap
- Plants and watering
- Outdoor lights
- Bathtub/overflow/enjoy
- Who you can call in a pinch?
  - Plumber
  - Electrician
  - Landlord
  - Neighbor
- Mail/paper
- Alarm system
- TV/video
- Laundry
- Thermostat

Information on housing

Address or addresses:

_____

_____

Directions to where you live:

_____

_____

_____

Alarm system? Company? Passwords and/or numbers?

_____

_____

_____

How do you retrieve your email and phone messages? How would your backup person retrieve them for you?

_____

_____

32

Notes: _____

_____

_____

Routine housing expenses

If you were absent for a length of time, how would routine bills be taken care of? Who would be responsible? Where would the money come from? What do they need to know?

Do you pay rent/mortgage? To whom? How much? When?

_____

_____

What are your regular expenses?

Utility bills _____

Insurance _____

Phone/cell phone _____

Cable/DSL _____

Loans _____

Other _____

CHAPTER FIVE

Be willing to laugh and keep things in perspective: This can be healing and leveling.
— Anonymous

Nitty-gritty of Your Life

A basic health history helps you, or someone helping you, whenever meeting a new health care provider or dealing with an emergency. Check with your doctor if you've questions about what to include.

Detail your health history

Any significant illnesses, conditions, surgeries?

_____

_____

_____

Allergies?

_____

_____

_____

Medications and schedules for taking them?

_____

_____

_____

Questions to ask your doctor: _____

_____

Why enlist help for medical appointments?

The thought of a friend or family member tagging along at your next doctor's appointment may cause you to feel embarrassed, fearful, or anxious. After all, why would you want your privacy invaded? Or why would you want to inconvenience the other person? However, there are times when you may want to consider taking someone along:

- If there is something major going on in your life
- If you are having trouble remembering details
- If you're embarrassed about some health issue and need support to communicate it accurately

Conditions to watch for or be aware of?

_____

_____

_____

Other data
Insurance company and ID number:

_____

Medicaid number:

_____

Medicare number:

_____

Social security or ID number:

_____

Emergency contacts 1 and 2:

_____

_____

Why you might not enlist help for medical-related visits

Why in the world would you not want to take someone else with you to a doctor's visit? You might not want to inconvenience someone else. Or you might want privacy. Less frequently acknowledged reasons might be wanting to tell only part of what's going on, embarrassment, or fear.

All of these reasons, of course, are valid. Still if there is something major going on in your life, having a backup at your doctor's appointment is a really solid idea.

35

Health-related insurances and records

Enlist a partner and, together, make your doctor's appointment efficient

1. Together brainstorm questions.

2. Know that you'll have a second set of ears to hear information and recommendations.

3. Increase your confidence in someone else being able to ask questions if you forget or if that person wasn't clear.

4. Enlist the other person to:
   - go with you whenever you go to the doctor.
   - read from your joint list.
   - write down answers.
   - be empowered to speak truth if you fudge or forget.
   - be authorized to ask questions, even if you are fearful or resistant at the moment.
   - advocate for your health and well-being.

If this person either holds your Durable Power of Attorney, or is in contact with that person, this increases their efficiency too.

Gather and store all health documents in one folder

1. **Health insurance** (include yes/no, company, contact and policy number)

   Health   ☐ Yes   ☐ No   ☐ Need

   Dental   ☐ Yes   ☐ No   ☐ Need

   Vision   ☐ Yes   ☐ No   ☐ Need

   Supplemental   ☐ Yes   ☐ No   ☐ Need

2. **Long-term care insurance**   ☐ Yes   ☐ No   ☐ Need

3. **Health savings account**   ☐ Yes   ☐ No   ☐ Need

4. **Disability insurance**   ☐ Yes   ☐ No   ☐ Need

36

Notes: _____

_____

Keep all your medical records together with *Medic Alert*.

Medic Alert is a premium service that can consolidate all of your health records in one place—directly from the source of the information (e.g. your doctor's office). Imagine having the ability to access your digital medical records online at any time, knowing that your documents are password-protected and securely encrypted with the latest technology.

5. In-home/assisted living insurance

    ☐ Yes   ☐ No   ☐ Need

6. Life insurance policies

    ☐ Yes   ☐ No   ☐ Need

7. Medic Alert program

    ☐ Yes   ☐ No   ☐ Need

8. Travel insurance

    ☐ Yes   ☐ No   ☐ Need

9. Health history, X-ray and lab results

    ☐ Yes   ☐ No   ☐ Need

10. Other

    ☐ Yes   ☐ No   ☐ Need

_____

_____

_____

_____

_____

Who knows where these policies are kept? Who has access to them?

Put copies of these, or at least the cover sheets, in your workbook.

Do you know who your beneficiaries are?

Be sure to update your legal documents as significant life events happen, or at least every 10 years.

Do you have an up-to-date list of all medications and supplements, along with dosages and schedules?

Why you need a Living Will

A Health Care Directive or Living Will is a legal document that lets you say what kinds of care you would or would not want if you were nearing the end of your life. Such things as CPR (emergency restarting of heart or breathing) and tube feeding (if you've lost the ablility to swallow), are covered.

Giving someone your Health Care Appointment, also called a Durable Power of Attorney for Health Care, or Healh Care Proxy, gives that person authority to make medical desicions for you if you cannot. It allows you to name the person: important if you have a partner to whom you are not legally married. It also gives you the chance to discuss what choices you'd want made. These are important conversations. It's also very good to clarify whether this person may step in immediately if you're in need or must wait until particular medical personnel are called in to certify your status. Different states have different laws about this, so it's important to check and be clear.

Health teams

It stands to reason that if your health providers act as a team they'll be better able to help you create and maintain the life you want.

Do you have any questions to ask?

1. Primary-care doctor and contact information:

_____

_____

2. Other medical specialists:

_____

_____

3. Other practitioners who assist with your health, such as naturopath, homeopath, etc.:

_____

_____

4. Is there one who's aware of ALL medications, supplements, and recommendations?

_____

38

Notes: _____

_____

Creating a health legacy

Particularly if you are living with someone, but not married, you will want to find out what laws pertain to you, whether your are over 65 or living in common law, or gay. Do you have a living will? Do you have someone appointed as having Power of Attorney (POA) in this arena? A backup? Do they know, and have you talked about your preferences and plans with them? Have you considered organ donation? Could your organs be for sale? There are options. For instance, some people use the Life Sharers Web site as one way to see that another organ donor would be the first to receive one of their organs. Think about what you want. Be clear! This is part of your legacy.

5. How about trainers/instructors/those who help keep you healthy?

_____

_____

6. Have you included eyes and teeth?

_____

_____

7. Who holds medical Power of Attorney (DPOA)?

Primary: _____

Secondary: _____

9. Do they all know about each other?

_____

10. Do you have

_____ ?

Gary, 76, was estranged from his children. He had strong opinions about the medical care he wanted and had communicated this to his partner, Betty. To ensure that she, not his kids, would be making decisions, he legally gave her his Health Care Power of Attorney.

Jan and Sue had been together for 12 years when Sue become very ill. When life-saving decisions needed to be made the doctors looked first to Sue's parents. Jan, however, had legal authority to speak for Sue. She stepped in, as Jan had asked.

39

Insurances

Today's insurance industry offers a lot of choices.

Do you have insurance? Do you have enough insurance? Is it time to make some adjustments?

Questions for your insurance provider:

Remember to regularly check beneficiaries.

_____

_____

_____

_____

What other types of insurance do you carry?

1. Home owner/rental/special riders:

_____

_____

2. Flood/earthquake:

_____

3. Umbrella:

_____

4. Business liability/consultation:

_____

Notes: _____

_____

_____

5. Auto/other vehicle:

_____

6. Other:

_____

_____

_____

In case of a natural disaster, what would I take?

_____

_____

_____

_____

Where would I go?

_____

_____

_____

Who else knows?

_____

_____

Finances and legalities

Miscellaneous documents

- Where do I keep my important papers? Is this a safe place? Who has access? Who knows?

- Do I have an accountant? Who? Where are my tax records?

_____

_____

_____

_____

_____

_____

_____

Organizing your assets

1. Banking

   ### Where is my bank? Is there more than one?

   Is there a particular person who knows me? Is there a local branch? What are the account numbers or the name of someone who knows?

   ### Savings accounts

   An institution where I have savings? For me? For my children's college? Other? Is there also a credit union?

   ### Safe deposits

   Do I keep a safe deposit box? Where is the key? Who is authorized to get in? What's in it? Do I have a fireproof safe in my house? Where is it?

   _____

   _____

   _____

2. Loans

   ### Do I have loans other than home loans?

   List them, however small; don't worry about the amount now, just list yes/no and to whom.

Notes: _____

_____

Employment records

- Employer and address?
- Name and contact for employer?
- Contract? Benefits?

Do I hold a mortgage on my home?

Or rent? Do I hold a mortgage for another property? Collect and add documentation or lease/rental agreements.

3. Investments

If I have investments, what and where are they? Is there anyone to contact? If I own real estate, where is it and who should be contacted? Any leases, loans, or mortgages?

Questions I have for financial services:

Questions I have for legal advisors:

Questions I have for my insurance agent:

43

Making use of your legal documents

To ease the burden on an executor and lessen the chance of any friction, you can specify in your will that the executor engage a neutral professional fiduciary.

Other legal documents

Power of Attorney

You will want to designate a trusted adult to hold the responsibility of being your Power of Attorney (POA). This is for legal or financial matters (so someone could pay bills, get items from a safe deposit box or such). You should also designate a backup person.

Do Not Resuscitate (DNR) form

A DNR form basically states that the named individual is not to be resuscitated if he or she stops breathing. If 911 is called, they must, by law, resuscitate, so if there is a DNR preference, then everyone around the individual must be informed so 911 is not called in.

Forms and legalities to consider

There are a variety of forms and legalities to consider when setting up a system that will optimally serve you or a loved one. First and foremost, put a WILL into place.

This is a way to deal with anything you may have acquired, to let people close to you know that you have thought of them, and to deal directly with estate-tax issues. Depending on your circumstances, you can work with a do-it-yourself will or go to an attorney. If anyone depends upon you, you must have a will.

With the advent of the Health Information Privacy Protection Act (HIPPA), regulations covering the legal bases have become even more important.

Designed to protect the privacy of health-care-related information, these HIPPA regulations can mean that even loved ones are kept at arm's length by health care systems or individuals who must obey the law. Thus it is necessary for a care partner to legally designate someone to whom such information can be given, by identifying to whom Health Care Appointment, or Health Care Power of Attorney, or Durable Power of Attorney is given. In meeting this requirement, a person gives written permission for a health care provider to share health care information with the designated individual. These legal steps are particularly important if you or the care partner lives alone, lives with an individual with whom there is not a legal marriage, or has no local family.

Notes:

44

Do you remember Karen Ann Quinlan?

One of several factors in determining the course of her life in a persistent vegetative state centered on legal guardianship and the fact that she'd not taken action to define who would make the final decision on her behalf.

Each legal form will probably need to be updated every few years, along with any insurance policies and beneficiaries.

The DNR and a Living Will (Advance Health Directive) need to be reasserted or reauthorized almost any time there is a hospitalization. The person holding Health Care Power of Attorney can accomplish this if the care partner is unable to do so.

Questions for lawyer and legal counsel:

_____

_____

_____

_____

_____

Burial and funeral wishes

These may include participation in the Neptune Foundation (they will cremate a body anywhere in the world and bring the ashes back to a designated place to be scattered) or, for instance, the Peoples Memorial Association, which will arrange for a low-cost funeral for a modest membership fee. Wishes related to organ donation should be clear. If you wish to donate, clarify if it's also OK for heirs or hospitals to sell organs.

Other legal documents

Marriage certificates/Adoption decrees/Divorce papers/Wills/Birth certificates/Driver's licenses/Passports/Citizenship papers or cards/Prenuptial agreements/Child custody arrangements/Certificates of domestic partnership/Licenses or accreditations: all should be accounted for and stored together. Just in case.

Keeping track of your business documents

Create a checklist

List documents to collect and insert here, or make and insert photocopies (and write down where the originals are kept).

	INCLUDED HERE	IRRELEVANT	COLLECT/ADD
Education	☐	☐	☐
Certifications and credentials	☐	☐	☐
Licenses	☐	☐	☐
Employees and partners	☐	☐	☐

46

Notes: _____

_____

_____

Co-workers are often the first to recognize a need. Balancing a person's privacy with the needs of a hierarchical organization and the chain of command for anything that impacts work can be very tricky. An early check with human resources is probably a good step in enlisting allies.

—John Gibson

	INCLUDED HERE	IRRELEVANT	COLLECT/ADD
Current resume	☐	☐	☐
Employer/s and contacts	☐	☐	☐
Contracts or agreements	☐	☐	☐
Business insurance (if you own)	☐	☐	☐
Disability insurance	☐	☐	☐
Other documents	☐	☐	☐

Perfect partners

If something happens to me, what happens to my company? It takes careful planning to create the kind of good partnerships that make for great business.

Bringing in a partner can add valuable new skill sets to a company, providing a quick way to jumpstart moribund growth or venture into a new market.

Small business owners are increasingly expected to bring in partners as part of their personal exit strategy as well as a way to ensure that their companies survive.

—excerpted from an article by Reed Richardson, *Priority Magazine,* May 2006

Serving your country

It's important to write the details of your national or military service. What you have done for your country matters greatly. Whether you've served in the military, the Peace Corps, AmeriCorps, Homeland Security assignments, or in another way, your service is important and should be documented.

Information to include:

- Branch(es) of service
- Dates and locations of service
- Discharge papers
- Awards or letter of commendation

_____

_____

_____

_____

_____

Document your military service

1. Tell your military story.

_____

_____

_____

_____

_____

_____

_____

Notes: _____

_____

In war, the voices of those who fight, heal or direct conflict are often isolated and distant from those who are sheltered from traumatic and life-changing events. How have participants in wartime events told their stories and how have they represented the events that surround them? [Stories told by those who were involved] contribute to the public dialogue about war through artwork that comments on or exposes their own experiences and perspectives. In effect, their art addresses the ways we remember and also participate in local, national, and international conflict.

—excerpt from Lesson 1, Wartime Voices,
Web site: www.pbs.org/art21/education/war/lesson1.html)

The soldier must be rooted in the past to understand the present so that he may project himself into the future.
—Dictionary of Military and Naval Quotations, Dept. of the Army

2. List any benefits due to you from this service.

_____

_____

_____

_____

3. List other service-related information or important contacts.

_____

_____

_____

_____

_____

_____

Entering the next stage of life

No matter where you are in life or how uncertain you are of exactly what's next (who really is?), you can start thinking about the next chapter in your life.

What is your legacy?

Most people say that the most important things in life are not financial. Family stories, values that have been passed along, the faith that someone has placed in them, the faith on which a life was based, cherished mementos: these are the legacies that seem to matter most. Yet fulfilling last wishes and distributing personal possessions, where there's ambiguity, are apt to bring forth conflict. Legacy planning is one way to maximize the positive and decrease the negative after you're gone. Whatever your age or stage, you can take time to write down, video, audio tape, or somehow capture what's important to you and your story so far.

Planning for tomorrow

Post-graduation plans (high school, college, military):

_____

_____

Dreams:

_____

_____

What will the time line be?

_____

_____

What are the challenges? The opportunities?

_____

_____

Notes: _____

_____

This pack rat has learned that what the next generation will value most is not what we owned, but the evidence of who we were and the tales of how we loved. In the end, it's the family stories that are worth the storage.
—Ellen Goodman

What will you be doing?

What does the next stage of life mean for you?

Will this next stage, at whatever age, mean another career? Jane Fonda has called the years after 60 a Third Act. Marc Freedman has called this time an Encore Career. Research shows that people at any age want flexibility and the opportunity to matter: even if you're nowhere near retirement, you may still identify with that. What does the next stage look like for you?

- Another career?
- More or different education?
- Mentoring?
- Volunteer work?
- Travel with a purpose?
- A blend of one or more of the above, or a sequence?

What will your life include?

- Personal growth and development
- Recreation
- Education
- Travel
- Starting a new venture
- Family
- Volunteer work
- Exercise and personal health
- Spiritual paths
- Writing a book

Next stage

In taking stock of my choices for the next stage of my life I will...

- Dream
- Read
- Talk to others
- Find a life coach
- Experiment
- Consult my experts
- Take a class
- Panic
- Take a nap
- Embark on *The Artist's Way* by Julia Cameron

Planning for retirement

Think also about your lifestyle, what is important to you, what sort of expenses you anticipate, and what income you wish to have. Balance this next to your current lifestyle and income.

With insurances, review beneficiaries. Consider naming individuals rather than leaving income to your estate, as this may be more advantageous for reasons of taxation. Keep the designations current. Review them at times of life changes: marriage, divorce, birth or adoption, retirement, or every 10 years. If you name a minor as beneficiary, be sure to name a custodian, too, to act on the child's behalf until he or she reaches adulthood.

Do have a savings account for emergencies! Get to know social security as best you can. In the December 2007 issue of *USAA Magazine*, the United States Automobile Association suggests going to the following Web site: ssa.gov/planners/calculators.htm and using calculator #2.

Notes:

Considering your options

If and when you plan to retire, experts recommend that you look beyond the trio of social security, Medicare, and Medicaid.

If you are part of a couple, you'll be wise to think about what financial resources you will have if the other person becomes incapacitated or unemployed, or leaves you through divorce or death.

Consider the following possibilities:

- ROTH IRAs
- CDs
- Annuities
- 401(k)s
- Investments
- Pensions
- 403 (b)s
- Savings accounts
- Insurances
- Federal government thrift savings plans
- Other income-producing activities (including work):
  - Commitments from children
  - Winning the lottery
  - Writing and publishing your memoirs
  - Other

_____

_____

_____

Items to be included in your legacy plan:

1. The gift of good records
2. The gift of good directions
3. The gift of history
4. The gift of yourself

53

Looking ahead to retirement living

If you were to stay at home, but were ill or incapacitated, who would care for you?

1. Child? Spouse?
2. Sibling? Friend? Team?
3. Someone appointed by DSHS?
4. Someone found by your Power of Attorney through an agency?
5. Would you have respite care?

Health concerns in retirement

If, for health reasons, you could not live at home, who would decide where you will live? What would you choose to do? Have you made any plans? Remember, 90 percent of those who are aging are cared for at home.

Where will caregivers come from?

_____

_____

If you are not at home, who will decide when and where you should live?

_____

_____

Where would the best community be? Have you looked?

_____

_____

54

Notes: _____

_____

_____

Living situations/choices

If, for health, age, financial, or social reasons, you cannot continue to live at home, what are your choices/wishes?

Move in with a relative or child? Have you asked? Could this change?

_____

Look to social service providers?

_____

Move early to progressive care?

_____

Hope that the timing is right for assisted living?

_____

Move to senior housing?

_____

Burial plans and preferences: Are these in place?

_____

_____

_____

_____

Do you have a preference regarding the commemoration of your life/funeral?

_____

_____

_____

CHAPTER SIX

Planning for Emergencies

Build an emergency kit. Plan what you'll need for yourself and your family if emergency responders can't reach you right away.

It's important to have an emergency plan in place for you and your family. Chances are, in an emergency you may not all be together. Make a plan and communicate that plan—along with your vital health information—to your emergency contacts.

- What do you need for yourself and your family if emergency responders can't help you during a disaster?

- Information on emergency kits are often available on your city's Web site (www.your city.gov/emergency) or on the Red Cross Web Site.

- A minimum three-day survival kit is a basic tool for peace of mind, comfort, and even survival during a disaster.

- Store at least one kit at home, in the car, and at work.

- Buy a starter kit or put one together yourself. If you buy a kit, remember to customize it to fit your needs. You may need extra items for children or pets.

- Identify a meeting place outside your home.

- Assign an out-of-area contact person who'll act as the communication hub.

The ICE Program (In Case of Emergency)

If you should ever become incapacitated because of an emergency, emergency workers need a quick way to find out who they should contact.

Paramedics, police, and firefighters sometimes waste valuable time trying to figure out which name in a cell phone to call when disaster strikes. They need to talk immediately to a family member or close friend so you can get the medical attention you need as soon as possible. Illinois Governor Blagojevich has successfully launched the Illinois ICE program. It could also be considerd a PSN (Personal Safety Net) program.

All you have to do is put the name of your emergency contact in your cell phone address book with the word "ICE" or "PSN" in front of it.

For example, if your emergency contact is Sheila, you should put "ICE–Sheila or "PSN–Sheila" in your cell phone book. That way, emergency workers treating you can quickly contact Sheila to get vital information about you. You can also have more than one emergency contact; just list them as ICE1, ICE2, and so on. It's an easy way to extend your safety net.

Notes:

It is vain to talk of the interest of the community, without understanding what is the interest of the individual.
—Jeremy Bentham

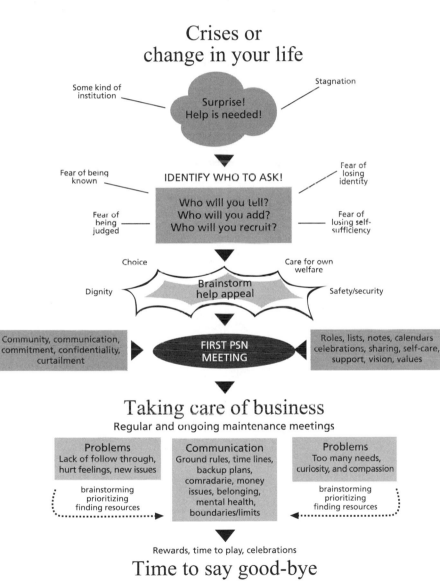

Crises or change in your life

Some kind of institution — Surprise! Help is needed! — Stagnation

Fear of being known — IDENTIFY WHO TO ASK! — Fear of losing identity

Fear of being judged — Who will you tell? Who will you add? Who will you recruit? — Fear of losing self-sufficiency

Choice — Brainstorm help appeal — Care for own welfare

Dignity — Safety/security

Community, communication, commitment, confidentiality, curtailment → FIRST PSN MEETING ← Roles, lists, notes, calendars celebrations, sharing, self-care, support, vision, values

Taking care of business
Regular and ongoing maintenance meetings

Problems
Lack of follow through, hurt feelings, new issues

brainstorming prioritizing finding resources

Communication
Ground rules, time lines, backup plans, comradarie, money issues, belonging, mental health, boundaries/limits

Problems
Too many needs, curiosity, and compassion

brainstorming prioritizing finding resources

Rewards, time to play, celebrations

Time to say good-bye

Get involved

Before a disaster, get involved and become familiar with community resources. These will be different in every city, but check out some that seem relevent to you.

- American Red Cross www.redcross.org
- Citizen Corps www.citizencorps.gov
- Volunteer agencies
- Police and fire departments
- Ambulance department
- Crisis clinic
- Family crisis services

You can also volunteer to develop site-specific disaster plans for your workplace, child's daycare center, or apartment building.

CHAPTER SEVEN

Pulling Your Team Together

Change can surprise and challenge us, whether the change is "positive" or "negative," whether it's a surprise or planned, change is guaranteed to rock our world.

In case of emergency

- STOP before you act! Take several deep breaths.
- RELAX as much as possible.
- ASK: who would you want to quickly talk this through with before taking action? Let your feelings out to get them behind you.
- BUILD a short-term plan.
- GATHER more data about what's happening and what options exist, with probable consequences of each.
- DEVELOP a longer-term course of action, including a team.

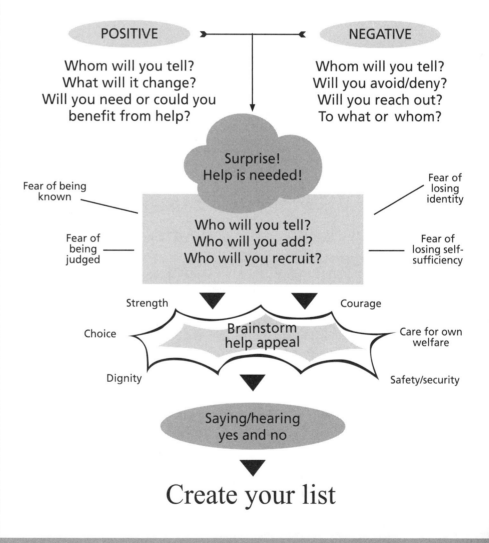

Change or challenge in your life

POSITIVE — Whom will you tell? What will it change? Will you need or could you benefit from help?

NEGATIVE — Whom will you tell? Will you avoid/deny? Will you reach out? To what or whom?

Surprise! Help is needed!

Fear of being known
Fear of being judged
Fear of losing identity
Fear of losing self-sufficiency

Who will you tell? Who will you add? Who will you recruit?

Strength · Choice · Dignity · Brainstorm help appeal · Courage · Care for own welfare · Safety/security

Saying/hearing yes and no

Create your list

Notes:

Five lessons from Personal Safety Nets:

1. Tell people what's going
2. Ask for help—early
3. Be specific in requests
4. Don't take "no" personally
5. Keep giving to others

Pulling your team together

Before the first meeting:

- Review your "A" and other safety net people lists.
- Meet with two of your best team members to determine:
    - Invitation
    - List
    - Location
    - Agenda
    - Goals

By the end of this first meeting, you hope to have the following:

- Roster of those who want to join in (remember not to take "no" personally!).
- A list of tasks and who will initially do them and for how long, and who will provide backup.
- A schedule for tasks and for the next meeting.
- A group mission or intention.
- Some ground rules for working together.
- A list of remaining questions or wishes.
- A good feeling about what's been accomplished.

Possible ground rules for the team

Start with these as examples to get your team going. Then include your own definitions of each, and enjoy writing your own ground rules:

- Maintain confidentiality (privacy).
- Set limits on your time and energy.
- Respect the time of each person.
- Keep money out of the relationships.
- Honor endings.
- Create your own.

Words to work by

*Choice, dignity,
respect, safety,
self-care, perspective*

*Truth walks toward us on the paths of our questions ...As soon as you think you have the answer, you have closed the path and may miss vital new information.
–Jacqueline Winspear,
Maisie Dobbs*

Using "people capital" wisely

We all want to be valued by those around us, seen in a positive light, and treated with respect. Further, most of us want to use our skills, talents, and time as efficiently and maximally as possible. In the team context, this often translates to scheduling, having a backup plan, and taking seriously our responsibilities to each other.

This is not at the cost of important human intersections or of interpersonal bonding. Nor does it ignore the social aspects of the team. Rather, it's centered on avoiding disorganization, redundancy, or confusion. It focuses on the needs of everyone involved. Whenever it's possible for team members to use strengths, skills, and time in ways that are fulfilling, individual team members will flourish to everyone's benefit.

Notes: _____

Tips for brainstorming

1. Start by defining the goal, problem, or question broadly and/or in several ways.

2. Everyone's input is valuable, and no ideas are excluded or too far out.

3. Keep notes. Have paper and markers at the ready.

4. After ideas on any given topic are generated, then prioritize and sequence. Take on tasks. Write down who'll do what, by when.

5. Create a plan and keep it doable. Come back to less essential parts or to those that come up along the way.

6. Have fun and build a stronger team through shared effort.

7. Create goals: What's the first action? What's most important? What is to be done now?

Sheldon Solomon, professor of psychology at Skidmore College, defines stress as when the demands on an individual are greater than the resources available to that individual. With time, education, and outside help, the stress level can change. Creating and using a safety-net team is one good way to decrease stress.

Pulling your team together

Our goal is to help you build a dependable team by communicating clearly and effectively.

Steps to having an effective team to support you or someone you care for:

1. Think and plan for who you think might be on your team.
   - How will you ask them?
   - What will you ask them for?
   - When will you ask?
2. Talk to these people.
3. Share your hopes, wishes, needs, plans, questions.
4. Communicate clearly (see pages 22-23).
5. Don't take "no" personally, and prepare to hear it sometimes.
6. Appreciate all support that comes your way—learn to see and acknowledge the small things too.

Join the team

Script for an emergency: Discussion example 1
Tony: single dad
Julie: 17-year-old daughter
John and Susan: Tony's friends

Tony: John and Julie, our daughter, Beth, has just been in a major climbing accident. You've been key members of my safety net, and now I'm asking you to help me form a care-share team to get through this terrible time. Will you help me pull together a team and give me direction?

Susan: Boy! How awful! We don't know why she went off to that godforsaken wilderness area to try her skills, but helping her and you through this now is the point. John and I'd be glad to help. Why don't we invite Carlos, and your friends Sylvia and Clay, to join in? They each have good strategizing skills and will contribute. Maybe we could meet here tonight after work. We can call for pizza and map out a plan.

Tony: That's wonderful. I'm scared and overwhelmed! I thought it was hard raising her as a little kid, but this teenage part often has me wishing that Rose were still here. I'll call the other three and make a list of things I hope to get help with.

Notes: _____

62

Discussion example 2:

Sarah: Beth, I would be happy to try to help you and Jim out while Julie is receiving her treatment. I'm so sorry that she's ill.

Beth: I can't tell you how much it means to me that you're there. Jim and I are trying to line up a number of people who can help. In this way we hope we won't have to ask too much of any of you.

Sarah: I think it's really wise of you and Jim to try to line up a whole team. I know that I'll have many time commitments with my part-time job and with the kids.

Beth: I know. Your plate is already full, and I feel bad about even asking.

Sarah: No, Beth, don't feel bad. What are friends for? I always want to know what's going on in your life, and I want you to ask me for help. I will always do what I can.

Beth: Well, Sarah, let's make a deal. First, Jim and I will do our best to recruit a large team to help protect all the members of the team. And, secondly, I'll promise to feel free to ask if you promise to always feel free to say "no." Is it a deal?

What does being a member mean?

- Being committed.
- Recognizing that at times you won't feel like helping or being there, but will choose to help and be there nonetheless.
- Being honest and caring.
- Knowing that you'll sometimes choose to say "no" for various reasons.
- Feeling good about participating.
- Being able to balance and rebalance your life and values while being a team member.
- Being healthier.
- Living longer.
- Being supported while helping.
- Asking for team support when something is hard for you while remembering that the primary focus of the group is not on you.
- Giving up control to benefit someone else.
- Offering support to other team members.

63

In each of our lives there is a time when we need others in a way we don't expect.
–Peter Grimm, MD

How could I use my safety net members?

Sometimes knowing what type of help we need or could accept allows us to better choose our personal safety net members.

Help with children
___Pick up or carpool
___Child-focused time
___Lunches
___Babysitting
___Other

Eldercare
___Company for elder
___Personal care
___Reading/TV time
___Other

Health/personal care
___Exercising/walking
___Nail care
___Shampoo/haircut
___Massages
___Other

Resource/delegating
___Medicare/Medicaid/Insurance
___Track MD visits
___Staying in touch
___Finding options
___Other

Meals
___Grocery shopping
___Cooking (delivering?)
___Helping with eating

Meals (continued)
___Dishes
___Other

Financial
___Bill/mail sorting
___Balancing statements
___Insurance papers
___Paying/tracking bills

Household chores
___Light house cleaning
___Windows/floors
___Cleaning refrigerator
___Laundry
___Other

Pets and plants
___Feeding and exercising
___Watering and trimming
___Mowing/trimming/raking
___Other

Telephone
___Calling to check in
___Medication reminders
___Telephone tree
___Other

Reading/writing
___Recording life story

Notes: _____

What help, guidance, or support do I need? What information would be helpful? Is a meeting the best way to get this?

Reading (continued)
___Reading books/papers
___Letters/cards/mail
___Other

Home repair
___Painting
___Closet/garage
___Moving
___Installing grab bars
___Other

Transportation
___To and from MD visits
___Shopping and errands
___Car maintenance
___Other

Medical
___Preparing for visits
___Accompanying
___Tracking details
___Other

Medications
___Remembering
___Procuring
___Coordinating
___Tracking
___Other

Friendly companionship
___Social outings
___Visits in hospitals
___Talking/visiting
___Personal shopping

Your own ideas:

_____

_____

_____

_____

_____

_____

_____

_____

Anticipating needs

Bill Gates Sr. added this endorsement to our book, *Personal Safety Nets.*

This is a really valuable book. The idea of anticipating the toughest personal or family tragedies by pre-arranging a support group is a wonderfully novel but practical idea. Beyond that the authors have provided an all-inclusive list of practical tips on how to do this effectively. I was particularly attracted to the wisdom of being sure that those you ask for help understand that you are perfectly willing to accept a "no" for an answer.

Hosting your first care-share team meeting

Telephone script for calling a care-share meeting for someone else

Hi, this is (name), and I'm calling you at the request of (name of care partner or care partner's significant other). As you know (name of care partner) has (describe circumstances that make the care-share team needed).

You have been an important part of (name's) life and we're happy you'll join in helping figure how to go through this situation. Many people have found that they are better able to meet challenges with the help of a care-share team. No one is expected to contribute or do any more than he or she is comfortable with.

We are planning on holding an initial information meeting on (two or three dates). Would you be able to attend?

Notes:

Written invitation to a first care-share team meeting

You're Invited!

Please come to hear more about what's going on with Julie and Tony, her dad.

September 11, 2008, 7pm-8:30pm
John & Susan's House
123 Main Street
Refreshments
RSVP to Susan 206.937.6543

Sharing is healing

When we tell our stories to one another, we, at the same time, find the meaning of our lives and are healed from our isolation and loneliness. Strange as it may seem, self-knowledge begins with self-revelation. We don't know who we are until we hear ourselves speaking the drama of our lives to someone we trust to listen with an open mind and heart.
—Sam Keen, *Your Mythic Journey*

Keep your team running smoothly

Below are brief pieces from discussions of understanding and agreements about teams.

The capacity of many to accomplish with ease what would have been extremely difficult or impossible for one or a few is illustrated by this example:

A retirement center needed to evacuate all residents after an ice storm shut off electricity. Ben couldn't walk. Fellow residents put a blanket under him, curled the corners, and shuffled along toward the exit. With ten of them together they all thought of the approach and found it easy to do.

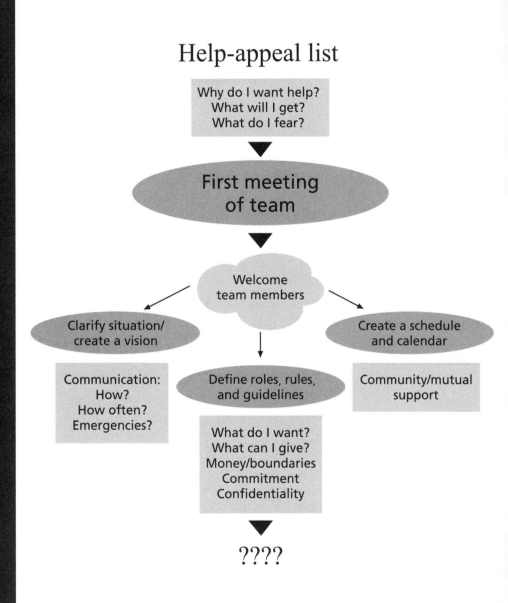

Help-appeal list

Why do I want help?
What will I get?
What do I fear?

↓

First meeting of team

↓

Welcome team members

Clarify situation/ create a vision

Communication: How? How often? Emergencies?

Define roles, rules, and guidelines

What do I want? What can I give? Money/boundaries Commitment Confidentiality

Create a schedule and calendar

Community/mutual support

↓

????

Notes:

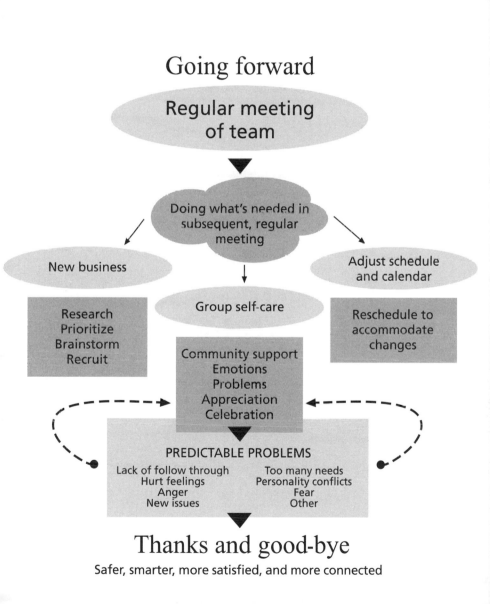

Going forward

Regular meeting of team

Doing what's needed in subsequent, regular meeting

New business

Research
Prioritize
Brainstorm
Recruit

Group self-care

Adjust schedule and calendar

Reschedule to accommodate changes

Community support
Emotions
Problems
Appreciation
Celebration

PREDICTABLE PROBLEMS

Lack of follow through
Hurt feelings
Anger
New issues

Too many needs
Personality conflicts
Fear
Other

Thanks and good-bye

Safer, smarter, more satisfied, and more connected

Personal safety

"[A personal safety net is] usually managed reactively, when there is little time for planning, etc. In a sense, [here is] ... a roadmap for contingency planning, the sort of planning that is 1) very important and

Before you say yes, ask yourself:

- Why would I like to help?
- Why wouldn't I want to do this?
- What would I get from saying yes?
- What would I worry about/ what would I fear? So, do I say yes or no?
- To all or some?
- With limits?

Why I might say yes to requests for participation/ assistance/help

- I like/love this person
- I was helped before
- To pay back
- Sense of duty
- Guilt
- Responsibility
- Can't back out

- I have the time
- I know it's manageable
- I like the others who will be helping
- I can do what I've been asked to do and I like it

What will I get out of saying yes?

How do I feel when I think about participating?

What scares, worries, or concerns me?

70

Notes:

2) needs to occur when [there is] time and other resources available to do it. Municipalities have contingency plans for earthquakes, floods, nuclear war, etc. But how many individuals have developed comparable plans for themselves?"

—Chad Lewis

Why I might say no to requests for participation/assistance/help

- I don't know the person well
- I don't like the others who are involved
- It feels overwhelming
- It's too far away
- I don't have time or energy
- I have too many other commitments

If you are declining, period, there are numerous ways to do so, with kindness and respect. If what you want is to be completely out of the loop, you might try something like this:

"I'm honored that you've asked, but it's simply that I'm not able to be part of this now. I wish you all the best as you go forward."

If you'd like to be in, later or for a different type of involvement, then you might try something like this:

- I'm not able to do that at this time.

- I'd rather not do that particular thing. Is there another?

- Just now I'm overcommitted, but please call back.

- I can't say yes to that, but how about ____?

- Here's something I'd like to offer. Would it be helpful?

- Could I be a backup person?

What can I offer?

> *"I firmly believe we all have the capacity to create our lives afresh all day long, and it's worth a try to recognize those small choice moments. I already am enjoying the chance to live creatively and intentionally minute by minute, as opposed to reactively. It seems well worth a try."*
>
> *—Sally B.*

Help with children
___Pick up or carpool
___Child-focused time
___Lunches
___Babysitting
___Other

Eldercare
___Company for elder
___Personal care
___Reading/TV time
___Other

Health/personal care
___Exercising/walking
___Nail care
___Shampoo/haircut
___Massages
___Other

Resource/delegating
___Medicare/Medicaid/insurance
___Track MD visits
___Staying in touch
___Finding options
___Other

Meals
___Grocery shopping
___Cooking (delivering?)
___Helping with eating

Meals (continued)
___Dishes
___Other

Financial
___Bill/mail sorting
___Balancing statements
___Insurance papers
___Paying/tracking bills

Household chores
___Light house cleaning
___Windows/floors
___Cleaning refrigerator
___Laundry
___Other

Pets and plants
___Feeding and exercising
___Watering and trimming
___Mowing/trimming/raking
___Other

Telephone
___Calling to check in
___Medication reminders
___Telephone tree
___Other

Reading/writing
___Recording life story

Notes: _____
_____
_____

Reading (continued)
___Reading books/papers
___Letters/cards/mail
___Other

Home repair
___Painting
___Closet/garage
___Moving
___Installing grab bars
___Other

Transportation
___To and from MD visits
___Shopping and errands
___Car maintenance
___Other

Medical
___Preparing for visits
___Accompanying
___Tracking details
___Other

Medications
___Remembering
___Procuring
___Coordinating
___Tracking
___Other

Friendly companionship
___Social outings
___Visits in hospitals
___Talking/visiting
___Personal shopping

Your own ideas:

_____

_____

_____

_____

_____

_____

_____

_____

_____

"When I had car trouble, one of them came to pick me up! When I had horrible news from my attorney, they all came to my side and listened as I cried and cried. Even when the news was unbelievable and shocking, and the only response was `I don't even know what to say,' they were there."

—Lisa P.

CHAPTER EIGHT

Maintaining Your Team

Leading, following, coordinating, and synergizing don't just happen. Careful planning and ongoing maintenance create great teams and extraordinary results.

There is an awesome power in collaboration as well as an increase in the collective I.Q.

- Gather nucleus of team
- Get to know one another
- Describe what's going on
- Ask and define questions
- Decide upon goal
- Prioritize
- Agree upon an action plan
- Celebrate community

Sample script for starting a first meeting

Thank you for coming to this meeting. And I want to start by thanking _____(the host). I'm really heartened and happy to see all of you here. It's good to know that we can work together to support _____(person who is being assisted).

There's a lot of information we want to cover. To help me as team leader for at least this first meeting, _____(team coordinator) has agreed to be the initial coordinator. Together we'll try to guide us all through this initial period.

Our first goals are to meet and to get to know one another, and to understand better what's going on for _____(person who is being assisted). Then we'll figure out what might be needed and how we can help meet those needs.

To get started, then, we'll send around a clipboard for you to write your name and contact information. As that's circulating, please, let's start to my left. Say your name and a little bit about what you currently do when you have leisure time and why you've come tonight.

Notes: _____

_____

_____

What if you can't do what you've said you'd do? Help! Life happens to me, too!
—Lisa Corbin

First meeting schedule

Without being fussy, check to see that the gathering space is warm and welcoming. It may help to be sure there are places for everyone you expect, and a lit candle or flowers.

As people arrive, pass out name tags. Be sure to take time for introductions and for each person to say why they've come. Circulate a sign-in/contact information sheet.

State again the reason for this meeting: to come to support _____ as a team. Ask everyone to answer these questions on a 3x5 card:

1. Why do you want to help _____?
2. What do you think you'll gain from this?
3. What concerns you about doing this?

Then share some answers, leaving the cards with the care partner.

Hear from the care partner (person being assisted) if he/she is present. Describe what's going on. Answer questions.

- List what needs to be done or is hoped for.
- Prioritize these needs/wants.
- See who can do what and brainstorm about meeting others.
- Create a beginning schedule and define a backup system.
- Schedule the next meeting.

Congratulate yourselves on what's been accomplished, share treats, say thank you to each other (even to those who've opted out) and to the care partner.

Important expectations

- Inclusivity: all are welcome.
- Respectful listening to all.
- Dealing with facts and truth, not rumors or assumptions.
- Honesty with self and what we can truly offer.
- Good faith efforts to reach consensus.
- Focus on goal of helping _____.
- Confidentiality.
- Honoring time together.

Gaining control in an information age

Know what you need to know and where to find it.

Handy people lists

- List of names, phone numbers, and backup phones for "A" team.

- List of same for "B" or "C" folks.

- Email list of these groups.

- Email list of folks to keep in the loop of information.

- List of names, addresses, phones of all of those above.

- List of physicians, resources used by care partner.

- List of medications and allergies of care partner.

- List of family members and pets.

- List of favorite places to go.

- List of what to pack to go there.

- Others.

Sample care-team member list

Date created: Team to assist:
(Update this at least quarterly and circulate updates to all.)

Name:
Address:
Home phone: Work phone:
Cell phone: Email:
(Underline preferred means of being contacted)
Special talents/gifts that you might offer:

Name:
Address:
Home phone: Work phone:
Cell phone: Email:
(Underline preferred means of being contacted)
Special talents/gifts that you might offer:

Name:
Address:
Home phone: Work phone:
Cell phone: Email:
(Underline preferred means of being contacted)
Special talents/gifts that you might offer:

Notes: _____

_____

_____

Sample calendar in the life of a care team

T	W	Th
Mary–pool		Dan–dinner
T	W	Th
Mary–pool	Sue–doctor	
T	W	Th
Mary–pool Bob–dinner		Lil–lunch

Important reminder:

To the person who waits, time is interminable and full of worries about what might have happened to you. Honor your commitments by being punctual, communicating schedule changes, and finding a replacement person to pick up for you if you cannot do what you thought.

It's important to alert people earlier rather than later if you discover or decide that you can't help.

Meeting check-in questions

Ongoing care-share team meeting

- **Create a welcoming space.**

- **Welcome people as they gather, but start on time.**

- **Ask each other a "check-in" question about relevant events or changes in commitments, or anything else that will increase the togetherness.**

  - What's one thing I especially like/enjoy/value about these meetings?
  - What's one success or good thing I've experienced since the last meeting?
  - What's a concern/problem/fear that I'd like to bring to this group? (If possible, communicate this to the team leaders ahead of time.)

- **Create an agenda that includes the following:**

  - Giving updates on changes in the care partner's needs/wants.
  - Addressing anything left over from the last meeting.
  - Brainstorming solutions.
  - Scheduling changes in needs or tasks.
  - Celebrating successes and enjoying one another.
  - Scheduling the next meeting.

- **Use a ritual to close the meeting (see appendix).**

Notes: _____

_____

_____

Learn from mistakes

- Let's try to identify the factors that contributed to Mary's not getting a ride home from her physical therapy appointment.

- Let's create a list of things to take when accompanying Fred to his oncology appointment so that next time he'll have what he needs.

- Let's brainstorm how to get new team members so we can have backups when one of us is sick next time.

- It's not who was at fault but rather what factors contributed to his bills not being paid. How can we assure that won't happen again?

- What went right since our last meeting? What went wrong since our last meeting?

- Because you are human, there will be mistakes. Though this may be unfamiliar, unwelcome, and/or unpleasant, it can help you learn something. There's a saying: "When the going gets rough, turn to wonder."

Ritual for closing a meeting

Light a candle in the middle of the space. Have a container nearby with slips of paper with each person's name on one piece. Draw one piece each, so that no one has his or her own name. Ask participants to write down or state something they appreciate about the person whose name they hold. When everyone's been recognized, extinguish the candle.

Great job!

You have done a very valuable thing for those who care about you. You can now model and spread the word about reimaging strength and developing your own team.

Celebrate small successes

- Brushing Sarah's hair makes her feel so much better and is such a wonderful thing you do.

- Writing the email message about Jim's upcoming surgery was so valuable.

- Picking Tim up after his soccer practice so I could meet with my attorney made such a difference.

- Walking Bill's dog and watering his plants took a lot of pressure off Bill.

- Calling every day of that awful week and leaving a brief, warm phone message was really thoughtful. It eased her mind.

What does your care-share team look like?

Any given care-share team will take on an identity that comes from the way in which it was formed, what it sees as its role, and the ways in which it functions. There is no right or wrong way to organize your team, but there are many different models. Is your care-share team more relaxed or scheduled? Is it made up of people who know, love, and were invited by the care partner? Or is it comprised of folks who belong to a parish, group, or temple that forms teams to help others? Maybe this continuum will help you learn more about your group and your options to create and modify a team that works for you.

loose and fluid	family or friends only
short-term	volunteers
as needed, "on call"	each one asked by you
one-to-one	only know the care partner

Notes: _____

_____

_____

80

Sample care manual for someone who's ill

- Health information
- Medications
- Schedule
- Contacts
- Care-share team
- Nutrition and transportation
- Other

Where is it all compiled?
Who knows where it is?
What is missing?

_____

_____

_____

_____

_____

wider community	tight and unchanging
paid assistance/assistants	long-term
group or point person who helps	scheduled for specifics
independent group of folks	collaborative

Do you and all your team members know what you need to know?

"The experience makes me especially thankful for friends, family, and this work that seeks to strengthen the bonds of community and hope for a more positive future. It strikes me that our collective, relational wealth really is the greatest asset we all have available to us."

— Bruce H.

Appendix Table of Contents

1. Getting Started: Beginning List of People, Plans, and Resources
2. "To Do" Reminders
3. Quick Start: The Power of Three
4. PSN Diagram With Example Categories
5. PSN Diagram for You or Someone You Help
6. My Personal "A" Team List and Contact Information
7. Brief PSN Personal Data Form
8. Personal Safety Nets® Wallet Card
9. Extended PSN Personal Data Form (PDF): Part 1
10. Extended PSN PDF: Part 2 – People
11. Extended PSN PDF: Part 3 – Secured Information
12. Listen to Your Experts: Key PSN Medical Information
13. Listen to Your Experts: Key PSN Insurance Information
14. Listen to Your Experts: Key PSN Financial Information
15. Listen to Your Experts: Key PSN Legal Information
16. Additional PSN Data for Current and Former Military Personnel
17. Surprise! Diagram of A Care-Share Journey
18. First PSN Team Meeting Schedule
19. Sample Ritual for the Beginning of the First Meeting
20. Helping: What Can I Offer To Do? My Time and Availability
21. Being Helped: What I Might Want and/or Need
22. Care Team Roster
23. Care-Share Team Calendar
24. Sample Rituals for Ending a Meeting
25. Sample Parent/Guardian Permission Form
26. Sample PSN PDF for Extended Travel
27. Sample Letter Recruiting Support for Someone Else
28. Workshop/Workbook Feedback

How we envision the appendix pages will be used:

Scan the appendix before getting serious. We've designed these sheets to help you go further or to compile your data into your own creative Personal Safety Net resource book. They are arranged sequentially to flow with the sections in this workbook.

We've included:
Samples
Examples
Forms

We encourage you to:

- *Fill these out*
- *Copy the pages*
- *Three-hole punch them*
- *Add them to your PSN (Personal Safety Net) binder along with cover sheets of insurance policies, passports, and other documents you want kept together, in your new fireproof safe or other secure place.*

Getting Started: Beginning List of People, Plans, and Resources

Knowledge is power: What do I know?

- Where are my important papers? The key to my safe deposit box? The password to my email address list? The spare key to my house? Who else knows this?
- Financial:
  – Bank/banker
  – Local branch
  – Credit union
- Insurance:
  – Life
  – Auto/home
  – Medical
  – Other
- Personal/Emotional: UNLESS THIS IS STRONG, THE REST MAY FALL APART.
  – Who are my friends? Who could I most likely count upon? To whom do/would I turn for various kinds of support? (Malcolm Gladwell's "Sympathy team")
  – ICE entries: Who'd be called first in an emergency? What would they need to know? Have I told them?
- Community:
  – Organizations that help or support me
  – Specific or categories of places I can/do turn to
- Spiritual:
  – My church/synagogue/mosque
  – What group inspires/supports me?
- Medical:
  – History
  – Current primary doctor
  – Allergies
  – Medications
- Legal:
  – Will
  – Ethical will
  – Plans for funeral
  – Affairs in order

The web of plans, resources, systems, and people who give meaning, support, and ease to my life.

Have I thought about?

"To Do" Reminders

Start now, and by this time next year you'll be done and only need to periodically revise!

What I need to do	By when	Done ✓
1.		
2.		
3.		
4.		
5.		
6.		
7.		
8.		
9.		
10.		

Quick Start:
The Power of Three

Who are the three people you can most count on for help?

(Fill in their names and how to contact them)

Name: _____

Phone numbers: _____

Address: _____

Email: _____

Name: _____

Phone numbers: _____

Address: _____

Email: _____

Name: _____

Phone numbers: _____

Address: _____

Email: _____

Does each one know that you count on them?

_____

_____

_____

Do they all know about each other so that they could team up and work together to help you?

_____

If not, what steps will you take to assure that they do know how to connect with each other?

_____

_____

PSN Diagram With
Example Categories

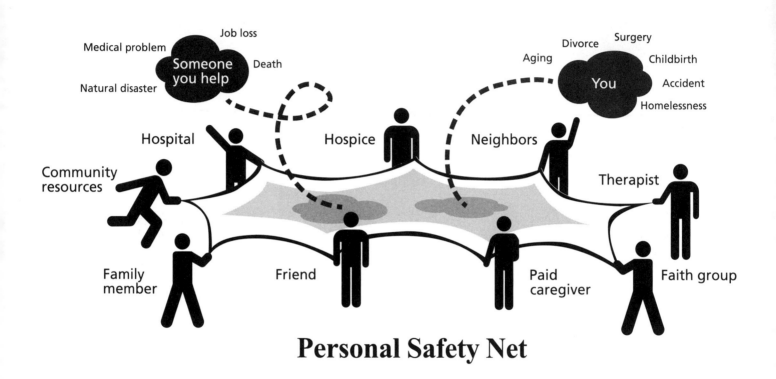

Personal Safety Net

PSN Diagram for You or Someone You Help

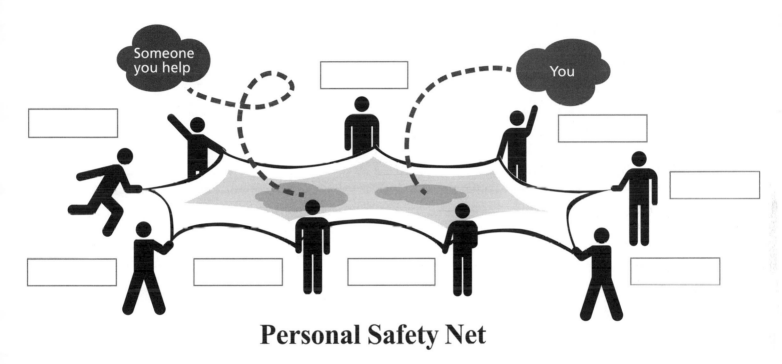

Personal Safety Net

My Personal "A" Team List and Contact Information

These are people whom I really count upon to help me.

Feel free to make copies of this and other pages for your personal use.

Name: ______________________________

Phone numbers: ______________________________

Address: ______________________________

Email: ______________________________

Name: ______________________________

Phone numbers: ______________________________

Address: ______________________________

Email: ______________________________

Name: ______________________________

Phone numbers: ______________________________

Address: ______________________________

Email: ______________________________

Name: ______________________________

Phone numbers: ______________________________

Address: ______________________________

Email: ______________________________

Name: ______________________________

Phone numbers: ______________________________

Address: ______________________________

Email: ______________________________

Name: ______________________________

Phone numbers: ______________________________

Address: ______________________________

Email: ______________________________

APPENDIX 6

Brief PSN Personal Data Form

Name: _____

Address: _____

Phone: _____   Email: _____

Who to contact first in case of emergency, and how to reach them?

_____

Who is the quarterback or point person of my personal safety net?

_____

_____

Where do I work or go each day? _____

Contact person there? _____

How to reach them: _____

My car (make, model and license number):

_____

Other members of my household (with phone numbers):

_____

Pets, (names, person who will care for them in an emergency/
veterinarian): _____

_____

Are there any other critical people or basic information that someone
would need in the event of an emergency involving me?

_____

Personal Safety Nets® Wallet Card

By filling and cutting this out you can keep this small information packet with you at all times.

Fold · Fold · Fold

My name is :

_____

and I'm creating this PSN card so that, if there's ever an occasion where I'm in need of help but can't arrange it, or reach out on my own, there will be a plan. If a decision MUST be made and I'm sick, injured, traveling or unavailable for other reasons I'd like to be known:

My birth date/place:

_____

Current address:

_____

_____

My personal safety net team – they know I count on them and know about each other. First call *(they have all the details)*

1. _____

_____

2. _____

_____

3. _____

_____

Primary care doctor:

_____

Phone:

_____

Hospital of choice:

_____

Phone:

_____

Prescriptions? *(list separately):*

_____

My Personal Safety Net

My name:

_____

(lower half — printed upside-down)

Seattle, WA 98116
4701 SW Admiral Ave. #126
Mail to:
www.PersonalSafetyNets.com
Personal Safety Nets®

_____

_____

_____

How to contact him/her:

_____

Who knows where my important documents are kept?

_____

_____

My Health Care Power of Attorney:

___ DNR order
___ Living will
___ Health Care Power of Attorney
___ A will
___ Attorney
Durable Power of
I have in place:

_____

_____

_____

Other?

_____

Spouse/partner?

_____

Business contacts:

_____

_____

If I have pets, they are:

_____

Keys?

Where are my car and house

_____

ID#:

_____

Insurance Company:

_____

Allergies?

Fold

Extended PSN Personal Data Form (PDF): Part 1

My name:_____

Birth date and Birthplace:_____

ID# (SS, DL, other):_____

Address: _____

Home and work:_____ Cell:_____

Email address: _____

I live alone? _____ Pets?_____ others?_____

First contact *(holds Power of Attorney)*:_____
Phone numbers:_____
Address: _____
Email: _____

Second contact *(alternate POA)*:_____
Phone numbers:_____
Address: _____
Email: _____

Other important contact: _____
Phone numbers:_____
Address: _____
Email: _____

Primary care doctor:_____
Phone: _____ Office location:_____
Medical identification numbers: _____
Insurance: _____
Allergies: _____
Prescriptions: *(list attached if needed)*_____
Hospital of choice: _____
Travel insurance if on a long trip:_____

Those listed below have access to my house and know where my other keys and data are located:

_____

_____

_____

Car: year, make, model, license number:

_____

_____

_____

Business partner or employer and contact information:

_____

_____

_____

Extended PSN PDF:
Part 2 – People

Family:
Parents' name
and contact
information

_____

_____

_____

Siblings

_____

_____

_____

Children

_____

_____

_____

In an emergency

PSN#1: How to contact? Relationship? City?

_____

PSN#2: How to contact? Relationship? City?

_____

PSN#3: How to contact? Relationship? City?

_____

PSN#4: How to contact? Relationship? City?

_____

Other close friends I could count on:

Friend #1–contact information, email:

_____

Friends #2–contact information, email:

_____

Friends #3–contact information, email:

_____

Business connections

Employer:_____ Phone: _____

Business:_____

Partner:_____

Phone and email: _____

Employee: _____

Phone and email: _____

Other business:

1. _____

2. _____

3. _____

Extended PSN PDF:
Part 3 – Secured Information

Insurances *(Copies of policies in this notebook. Originals in safe-deposit box.)*

Home–Company, policy # and phone contact #

_____

Auto–Company, policy # and phone contact #

_____

Umbrella–Company, policy # and phone contact #

_____

Health–Company, policy # and phone contact #

_____

Health–Medic Alert: policy # and phone contact #

_____

Life Company, policy # and phone contact #

_____

Business–Company, policy # and phone contact #

_____

Disability–Company, policy # and phone contact #

_____

Burial–Company, policy # and phone contact #

_____

Long-Term Care–Company, policy # and phone contact #

_____

Finances
Accountant:_____
Banking:_____
Business #1:_____
Mail to:_____
Business partner or employer:_____
Business #2:_____
Legal:
  Personal:_____
  Business:_____

Real Estate
Principle residence address:

_____

_____

Owned? Rented?

_____

Family home owned by:

_____

Any other important info:

_____

_____

Any other real estate:

_____

_____

_____

_____

Listen to Your Experts:
Key PSN Medical Information

Here is a partial list of those who might be seen as resources.

- *Lawyer*
- *Insurance agent*
- **Case manager**
- *Banker*
- *Trust officer*
- **Therapist**
- *Probation officer*
- **School specialist**
- **Physicians**
- *College advisor*
- *Work reference*
- *Mentor*
- *Employer*
- *Coach*
- *Parole officer*
- *???*

Your various professional advisors can be important collaborators in your personal safety net. Tell them about what you are doing and enlist their assistance as you create a safe and secure world for yourself and those you love.

We believe that you would benefit from discussing with your medical advisor what medical information is important to collect and have available. Also, where should this information be stored and how, and by whom, can it be accessed when needed.

Jot down your questions, ideas, notes and thoughts to take with you and discuss with your medical advisor below:

Listen to Your Experts:
Key PSN Insurance Information

Your various professional advisors can be important collaborators in your personal safety net. Tell them about what you are doing and enlist their assistance as you create a safe and secure world for yourself and those you love.

We believe that you would benefit from discussing with your insurance advisor what insurance information is important to collect and have available. Also, where should this information be stored and how, and by whom, can it be accessed when needed.

Jot down your questions, ideas, notes, and thoughts to take with you and discuss with your insurance advisor below:

_____

_____

_____

_____

_____

_____

_____

_____

_____

_____

Here is a partial list of those who might be seen as resources.

- *Lawyer*
- **Insurance agent**
- *Case manager*
- *Banker*
- *Trust officer*
- *Therapist*
- *Probation officer*
- *School specialist*
- *Physicians*
- *College advisor*
- *Work reference*
- *Mentor*
- *Employer*
- *Coach*
- *Parole officer*
- *???*

Listen to Your Experts:
Key PSN Financial Information

Here is an incomplete list of those who might be seen as resources, depending on you and your life:

- *Lawyer*
- *Parole officer*
- *Insurance agent*
- *Case manager*
- **Banker**
- **Trust officer**
- *Therapist*
- *Probation officer*
- *School specialists*
- *Physicians*
- *College advisor*
- **Work references**
- *Mentors*
- **Employer**
- *Coach*
- *???*

We view your various professional advisors as being important or essential collaborators in creating and maintaining your personal safety net. Tell them about what you are doing, and enlist their assistance in helping you create the most safe and secure world for yourself and those you love.

We believe that you would benefit from discussing with your financial advisor what financial information is important to collect and have available. Also, where should this information be stored and how, and by whom, can it be accessed when needed.

Jot down your questions, ideas, notes and thoughts to take with you and discuss with your financial advisor below:

_____

_____

_____

_____

_____

_____

_____

_____

_____

_____

Listen to Your Experts: Key PSN Legal Information

Your various professional advisors can be important collaborators in your personal safety net. Tell them about what you are doing and enlist their assistance as you create a safe and secure world for yourself and those you love.

We believe that you would benefit from discussing with your legal advisor what legal information is important to collect and have available. Also, where should this information be stored and how, and by whom, can it be accessed when needed.

Jot down your questions, ideas, notes and thoughts to take with you and discuss with your legal advisor below:

Here is a partial list of those who might be seen as resources.

- **Lawyer**
- _Insurance agent_
- _Case manager_
- _Banker_
- _Trust officer_
- _Therapist_
- **Probation officer**
- _School specialist_
- _Physicians_
- _College advisor_
- _Work reference_
- _Mentor_
- _Employer_
- _Coach_
- **Parole officer**
- _???_

Additional PSN Data for Current and Former Military Personnel

Does filling out this sheet bring to mind others you wish to maintain connection with? Who?

_____

_____

_____

_____

How can you establish/ maintain that connection?

_____

_____

_____

_____

When will you do this?

_____

_____

_____

Name:

Home address:

Home phone:

Email:

Military Service

Armed forces: Date of discharge:

Branch of service:

Dates of service:

Proof of MIA notification:

National Guard

Dates of service: Date of discharge:

Active duty:

Active Reserves

Dates of active duty: Date of discharge:

Have you ever been awarded a Purple Heart or incurred a service-related disability?

List military awards or special recognitions:

Surprise! Diagram of a Care-Share Journey

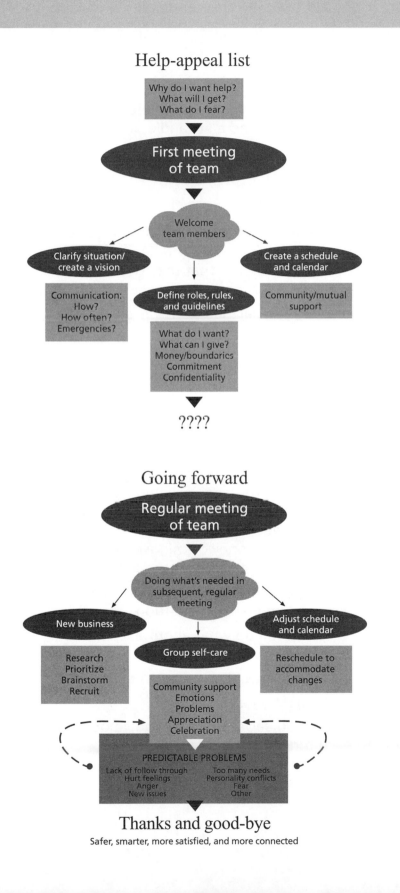

Help-appeal list

Why do I want help?
What will I get?
What do I fear?

First meeting
of team

Welcome
team members

Clarify situation/
create a vision

Create a schedule
and calendar

Communication:
How?
How often?
Emergencies?

Define roles, rules,
and guidelines

Community/mutual
support

What do I want?
What can I give?
Money/boundaries
Commitment
Confidentiality

????

Going forward

Regular meeting
of team

Doing what's needed in
subsequent, regular
meeting

New business

Adjust schedule
and calendar

Research
Prioritize
Brainstorm
Recruit

Group self-care

Reschedule to
accommodate
changes

Community support
Emotions
Problems
Appreciation
Celebration

PREDICTABLE PROBLEMS
Lack of follow through   Too many needs
Hurt feelings   Personality conflicts
Anger   Fear
New issues   Other

Thanks and good-bye
Safer, smarter, more satisfied, and more connected

First PSN Team Meeting Schedule

- Without being fussy, check to see that the gathering space is warm and welcoming. Some things that can help are having a place for everyone you expect to come and a lit candle or flowers.

- As people arrive, unless everyone is already acquainted, have name tags. Be sure to take time for introductions and for each person to say why they're present.

- State the reason for this meeting: to come together to assist _____ during this time of _____. Ask everyone to tell a little about their reason for having come and have someone record this information. Alternatively, ask that they write this down on a piece of paper and collect for the care partner to read later. (Ritual #1)

- Hear from the care partner, if he/she is present.

- Talk about what needs to be done, who can do what, and create some sort of schedule.

- Speak of expectations and set some ground rules. Here are some examples:
  - Be inclusive. Respectfully hear everyone.
  - Try to deal with facts and truth, not rumors or assumptions. Stay honest with offers and feelings.
  - Give a good faith effort at reaching consensus.
  - Stay focused on the goal of being helpful. Stay away from the past or side issues.
  - Maintain confidentiality.
  - Don't exchange money or things of value.
  - Honor your time together in some way.

- List tasks or issues that need to be addressed. Prioritize to pinpoint those that need immediate attention. Focus here first.

- Decide who can/will do what about each immediate item, and by when. Write this down.

- For what remains, brainstorm how the need might be met.

- Schedule the next meeting.

- Congratulate yourselves on what you've done, share treats, say thank you to each other and your care partner.

Sample Ritual for the Beginning of the First Meeting

Step one:
- Pass out note cards and pens.

Step two:
- Have all present write down the answers to four questions, numbering their answers:
    - Why have you come?
    - What are you feeling now?
    - Why do you want to help _____ (care partner)?
    - What do you think you will get out of heping?

Step three:
- Depending on the group, choose one of the following, or make up a variation of your own:
    - In a circle, read aloud what's been written.
    - Randomly exchange cards and read what someone else wrote.
    - Collect cards in a hat, box or other container. Have a leader read these aloud to the care partner and the group.
    - Pass the cards to the care partner, for him/her to read later.

This ritual or practice has the main purpose of letting the care partner know how she/he figures in the lives of those who have gathered to be part of this care team. When times are tough, this collection may be really helpful.

Helping: What Can I Offer to Do?
My Time and Availability

Help with children
___Pick up or carpool
___Child-focused time
___Lunches
___Babysitting
___Other

Eldercare
___Company for elder
___Personal care
___Reading/TV time
___Other

Health/personal care
___Exercising/walking
___Nail care
___Shampoo/haircut
___Massages
___Other

Resource/delegating
___Medicare/Medicaid/
   Insurance
___Track MD visits
___Staying in touch
___Finding options
___Other

Meals
___Grocery shopping
___Cooking (delivering?)
___Helping with eating
___Dishes
___Other

Name: _____

Address: _____

Phone: _____ Email: _____

Availability: What are the best days and times for giving help?

_____

Time/Day	Mon.	Tues.	Wed.	Thurs.	Fri.	Sat.	Sun.
Mornings							
Afternoons							
Evenings							
Varies							

Financial
___Bill/mail sorting
___Balancing statements
___Insurance papers
___Paying/tracking bills

Household chores
___Light house cleaning
___Windows/floors
___Cleaning refrigerator
___Laundry
___Other

Pets and plants
___Feeding and exercising
___Watering and trimming
___Mowing/trimming/raking
___Other

Telephone
___Calling to check in
___Medication reminders
___Telephone tree
___Othe

Reading/writing
___Recording life story
___Reading books/papers
___Letters/cards/mail
___Other

Home repair
___Painting
___Closet/garage
___Moving
___Installing grab bars
___Other

Transportation
___To and from MD visits
___Shopping and errands
___Car maintenance
___Other

Medical
___Preparing for visits
___Accompanying
___Tracking details
___Other

Medications
___Remembering
___Procuring
___Coordinating
___Tracking
___Other

Friendly companionship
___Social outings
___Visits in hospitals
___Talking/visiting
___Personal shopping

Being Helped:
What I Might Want and/or Need

Help with children
___Pick up or carpool
___Child-focused time
___Lunches
___Babysitting
___Other

Eldercare
___Company for elder
___Personal care
___Reading/TV time
___Other

Health/personal care
___Exercising/walking
___Nail care
___Shampoo/haircut
___Massages
___Other

Resource/delegating
___Medicare/Medicaid/
   Insurance
___Track MD visits
___Staying in touch
___Finding options
___Other

Meals
___Grocery shopping
___Cooking (delivering?)
___Helping with eating
___Dishes
___Other

Financial
___Bill/mail sorting
___Balancing statements
___Insurance papers
___Paying/tracking bills

Household chores
___Light house cleaning
___Windows/floors
___Cleaning refrigerator
___Laundry
___Other

Pets and plants
___Feeding and exercising
___Watering and trimming
___Mowing/trimming/raking
___Other

Telephone
___Calling to check in
___Medication reminders
___Telephone tree
___Other

Reading/writing
___Recording life story
___Reading books/papers
___Letters/cards/mail
___Other

Home repair
___Painting
___Closet/garage
___Moving
___Installing grab bars
___Other

Transportation
___To and from MD visits
___Shopping and errands
___Car maintenance
___Other

Medical
___Preparing for visits
___Accompanying
___Tracking details
___Other

Medications
___Remembering
___Procuring
___Coordinating
___Tracking
___Other

Friendly companionship
___Social outings
___Visits in hospitals
___Talking/visiting
___Personal shopping

Care Team Roster

Date created or updated:

_____

Care team in support of:

_____

_____

Care partner's address, phone number:

_____

_____

_____

_____

Leader/facilitator:

_____

Recorder:

_____

Other roles that are specified:

_____

_____

Members

Name: _____

Phone: *day and night, cell phone if appropriate*

_____

Address: _____

Email address: _____

Relationship to care partner: _____

Name: _____

Phone: *day and night, cell phone if appropriate*

_____

Address: _____

Email address: _____

Relationship to care partner: _____

Name: _____

Phone: *day and night, cell phone if appropriate*

_____

Address: _____

Email address: _____

Relationship to care partner: _____

Care-Share Team Calendar

Week _____

Sunday	Monday	Tuesday	Wednesday	Thursday	Friday	Saturday

Care-share team	Work phone	Home phone	Email
1.			
2.			
3.			
4.			
5.			

Medical information for care partner

Name/address _____

_____

SS # _____

Birth date _____

Blood type _____

Allergies _____

Medications _____

Emergency numbers for care partner

Main doctor _____

Power of Attorney (POA) _____

POA for Health _____

Family member _____

Insurance _____

Sample Rituals for Ending a Meeting

Ending a meeting

Light a candle in the middle of the space. Have a container with slips of paper with each person's name on one piece. Draw one piece each so that no one has his or her own name. Ask each person present to state something they appreciate about the person whose name they have drawn. When everyone has been acknowledged, extinguish the candle.

Moving in

When moving in, proceed from space to space with a lit candle, say in each space what you hope will happen or be felt there. In an entry–that good friends and people will enter and share the warmth of the place; in a sitting area–that people will gather and be enriched by the experience; and so on. At the end of the journey extinguish the candle.

Sample Parent/Guardian Permission Form

Date _____

To whom it may concern:

We hereby give permission for _____
(list whomever is being authorized to travel with minors; include full name, address, and contact numbers below) to travel with and obtain any necessary medical care for _____
(list names and birth dates of relevant minors) during travels to the following places _____
(list destinations and dates of travel there).

_____

_____
Parent "A" print name   Signature

Contact information: _____

_____

_____
Parent "B" print name   Signature

Contact information: _____

_____

In some cases, this may need to be notarized.

Consult with your legal advisor.

_____

Relevant information:
(list allergies, vacation)

_____

_____

_____

_____

_____

_____

Family contact people:

- Jan Ames (Susie's sister)
  Address, phone & email
- Ann Doe (Sarah's sister)
  Address, phone & email

Seattle contact people:

- John Baker (Sue's business partner: picks up mail)
  Address, phone & email
- Pat Lee (friend; well connected with RV community...) can help find us in an emergency
  Address, phone & email
- Karen Path, MD
  (doc for us both)
  Address, phone & email
- Health insurance: Your BlueShield (copies of plan/cards attached)

Seattle financial people:

- Banker, branch, phone, email
- Bookkeeper, address, phone, email

Renters:

- (house keys attached): names, address, phone, email

Storage Unit and Mail Box:

- (keys attached): locations, codes, phone numbers

Vendors for house maintenance:

- general, plumber, roof, yard, electrician, water filter

Sample PSN PDF for Extended Travel

| Susie Que Jones | Born 5/5/75 | SS #654-21-9987 |
| Sarah Bee Smith | Born 12/12/74 | SS #123-44-5567 |

Contact info:

- Email: s.jones@comcast.net, regular email account; accessible only when we have Internet access.
- Phone #: 206-999-4567, messages will be checked as able, but this will be spotty.
- ABCtravelmail@snowbirds.com: Best way to reliably reach us, but keep messages short and text only; no attachments, no extra line spaces or extra paragraph returns (new lines). If replying to our mail, do not hit "reply." Start a new message, so our message isn't attached.
- Visit our website: www.SusieandSarah@website.com.
- Other: We also will have a satellite phone and a "Skype" account (voice-over Internet program) that we can use to make phone calls. We can reach you this way. We will let you know if you can reach us!

Emergencies:

- In case of life-threatening emergency if unreachable, our RPIRB (Emergency Position-Indicating Radio Beacon) will be activated, contacting the closest search and rescue organizations. If they can't find us, Sue's sister (Jan Ames) & Sarah's sister (Ann Doe) will be contacted.
- When we're out of range, we will email Judy, Jan, and/or Ann at least weekly so people will know our whereabouts and ETAs. If no one hears from us for more than a week, contact state patrol: 707-826-7132, www.snowbirds.com. This is a network of RVers and land-based HAM operators. We'll check in on a regular basis; they can help locate us.
- RV description: s/v Our Rig: length, license, colors. Hometown: Seattle, WA; HAM call-sign: JC4JCG.

Sample Letter Recruiting Support for Someone Else

News of Mom, Teresa R. Mason

Dear Friends,

Since September 5, 2007, Teresa has become a resident of the Kildeer Community in Lincoln, FL. Both a retirement and an assisted living facility of nearly 100 residents, Kildeer has recently moved to a new building located at 725 E. Jefferson St, Lincoln, FL, 80123. Mom's unit is #712 and her new phone number is (333) 567-7891. I know she'd be happy to have a phone call or visit from you. Because of her extremely poor eyesight, all of her mail is directed to me in Canyondale, AZ, so cards and letters are of little value to her.

Though it was no small task to move from her home of 55 years, Mom seems to be adapting nicely to her new surroundings. She's pleased to have people with whom to interact daily at meals, exercise class, worship services, and the many other activities that are provided for the residents. According to her, the meals are delicious and she loves the staff. Quite a few know her from the time that her sister, Betty Bosh, was a 10-year resident of the old Kildeer facility on "A" Street and Mom used to visit there. Her two-room unit plus bath and kitchenette is comfortable with plenty of light and a nice view of the expansive lawn and the activity of South Hill Road. She brought her favorite furniture and pictures, so it seems very much like "home" to her.

If you choose to phone her or visit in person, I'd like to remind you that her vision and hearing are extremely poor. Additionally, over the past few years, she has begun to suffer from the onset of dementia (very few don't who reach the age of 92!). It may take her awhile to recognize you, but please don't be offended. Occasionally, she has a bit of trouble recognizing my sister (Terri Green) and me. In due course, she'll remember you, and even if she doesn't, she'll be glad to have a caller.

If you have any questions or concerns, please don't hesitate to call me at (890) 987-9876 or email me at yourmail@provider.net. We appreciate that you have been an important part of Mom's life.

Warmly,
Ben

Workshop/Workbook Feedback

Date:

_____

_____

Presentation:

_____

_____

This workbook has been developed in collaboration with individuals and groups. We depend upon your feedback to keep it relevant and useful. Gold stars to all who participate with a reply!

1. What did you like best about today's workshop?

2. What did you like least?

3. What's most valuable about the workbook?

4. How can we improve the workbook?

5. Is there anything you would add?

6. Anything else you feel will help make *Personal Safety Nets* more valuable to more people?

7. How did you hear about this workbook or workshop?

8. If you'd like to receive our monthly email newsletter, please give us your email address.

Please mail us this sheet to: 4701 SW Admiral Way #126, Seattle, WA 98116 and/or email us through our Web site www.PersonalSafetyNets.com with any additional suggestions on how to make this workbook more valuable to you and those you serve.

How to Order a Personal Safety Nets® Book or Workbook

To purchase, visit our Web Site: www.PersonalSafetyNets.com
Or to order an autographed copy send the below order form to:

Safety Nets Unlimited
Mail to: 4701 SW Admiral Way #126, Seattle, WA 98116
[p] 206-933-6577   [f] 206-935-0539
Checks payable to: Personal Safety Nets (PSN)

Prices:	Price	# of Copies	Total Price
Personal Safety Nets® Book: Getting Ready for Life's Inevitable Changes and Challenges			
Hardback edition	$29.95	_____	_____
Paperback edition	$17.95	_____	_____
Audio CD	$15.00	_____	_____
Personal Safety Nets® Workbook: Get Ready/Get Started			
Workbook	$17.95	_____	_____
	Total cost of items		_____
	WA residents add applicable tax		_____
	Shipping & handling: 1 item = $5.00, additional @ $2.00		_____
	Total order		_____

Name: _____

Address: _____

City: _____ State: _____ Zip code: _____

Phone: _____ Email: _____

Credit card #: _____ Exp. date: _____

Signature: _____

- For gifts, special instructions, or shipping to a second address, please attach additional sheets to this order form. Gift cards available, with your own message, for $.50 each.

- To process your credit card, you must include mailing address and phone number.

Ideally suited for life's changes and challenges: Birthdays, weddings, new babies, retirement, empoyee thank-yous, extended travel, illness, and book groups. Thank you for ordering from us.